Writers Uncovered

PHILIP PULLMAN

Vic Parker

www.heinemann.co.uk/library
Visit our website to find out more information about Heinemann Library books.

To order:
☎ Phone 44 (0) 1865 888066
📄 Send a fax to 44 (0) 1865 314091
💻 Visit the Heinemann bookshop at www.heinemann.co.uk/library to browse
our catalogue and order online.

British Library Cataloguing in Publication Data
Parker, Vic
  Philip Pullman. – (Writers uncovered)
  823.9'14
A full catalogue record for this book is
available from the British Library.

Editorial: Charlotte Guillain and Dave Harris
Design: Richard Parker and Q2A Solutions
Picture research: Hannah Taylor and Bea Ray
Production: Duncan Gilbert

Originated by Chroma Graphics (O) Pte Ltd.
Printed and bound in China by
  South China Printing Company

10 digit ISBN: 0 431 90629 7
13 digit ISBN: 978 0 431 90629 4

10 09 08 07 06
10 9 8 7 6 5 4 3 2 1

Acknowledgements
The publishers would like to thank the
following for permission to reproduce
photographs:
Advertising Archive p. 9; Alamy Images
p. 13 (Oxford Picture Library); ArenaPAL
p. 39 (Marilyn Kingwill); Bridgeman Art Library
pp. 12 (Fitzwilliam Museum, University of
Cambridge, UK), 14 (Private Collection,
© Agnew's, London, UK); Camera Press
pp. 23 (Eamonn McCabe), 42 (Ian Lloyd);
CILIP p. 36; Corbis p. 20 (Adam Wollfitt);
David Fickling Books p. 19; Eastern Evening
News p. 6; Empics/PA p. 37; Fremantle
Media p. 22; Getty Images p. 21 (Dorling
Kindersley); Mary Evans Picture Library p. 7;
National Maritime Museum p. 8; Oxford
University Press p. 16; Philip Hollis p. 38;
Polka Theatre pp. 15, 17; Puffin p. 10;
Random House pp. 27, 29, 31; Rex Features
pp. 24 (Francesco Guidicini), 4 (Sutton-
Hibbert); Scholastic pp. 18, 33, 35a, 35b,
35c; Ysgol Ardudwy School p. 11.

Every effort has been made to contact
copyright holders of any material reproduced
in this book. Any omissions will be rectified
in subsequent printings if notice is given to
the publishers.

The paper used to print this book comes
from sustainable resources.

CONTENTS

Words appearing in the text in bold, **like this**, are explained in the glossary.

There is no other modern author who has written such a variety of books as Philip Pullman. Among the wealth of his work are **graphic novels**, plays, fairy stories, **mythic** tales, Victorian **melodrama**, **gothic horror** stories, and **contemporary** novels. He has also written a hugely imaginative **trilogy** which has instantly become a modern classic and won him fans from all over the world.

Most writers' work appeals only to certain groups of people, such as children or adults, boys or girls. However, Philip's books have crossed all the usual boundaries and are cherished by readers of all ages and both sexes. His stories have sold millions of copies worldwide and have won many awards.

This is the face behind the stories.

Why do readers love Philip Pullman stories?

Philip's stories are crammed full of atmosphere, hair-raising plotlines, captivating characters, attention-grabbing drawings, thought-provoking ideas, and references to other books and writers. His tales are action-packed, full of nail-biting suspense and cliffhangers. They are hugely unpredictable: the "goodies" often die and the "baddies" often get off without being caught.

If you dive into a Philip Pullman book, you cannot begin to guess what lies in store, but you can be certain you are off on a breathtaking adventure.

FIND OUT MORE...

Here are some of Philip's favourite things:

Favourite TV show...	*Sergeant Bilko.*
Favourite movie stars...	Laurel and Hardy.
Favourite poem...	As a child, Philip loved the poem *Invictus* by W E Henley – it made him feel proud and courageous.
Favourite sport...	Philip likes sport – but he prefers watching it on television rather than doing it himself.
Favourite hobbies...	Drawing, making things from wood, playing the piano.
Favourite music...	Philip loves all kinds of music – classical and jazz in particular. He cannot have music playing while he is writing as he finds it distracting, but he likes listening to music if he is drawing or woodcarving.

Philip Pullman was born in Norwich on 19 October 1946. His mother was called Audrey and his father was called Alfred. The couple soon had another son, who they named Francis.

Travels abroad

Philip's father was an RAF fighter pilot. His job took him all around the world, and the family moved with him from airbase to airbase. Philip and Francis did not see much of their father, because he was often away on flying missions.
However it was a terrible shock when Alfred was killed in a battle in Kenya, when Philip was just seven.

INSIDE INFORMATION

The main characters in Philip's stories are often without one or both of their parents. For instance, in *The Firework-Maker's Daughter*, Lila lost her mother when she was young, and in *The Ruby in the Smoke*, Sally Lockhart is a sixteen-year-old orphan.

This photo was taken when Philip collected a medal from the Queen at Buckingham Palace with his mother and brother. The medal was called a Distinguished Flying Cross, and it was awarded to Philip's father after he died.

Inspiring storytellers

Back in Britain, Philip's mother found a job in London. Her cramped **lodgings** and long working hours meant it was better for the boys to live with their grandparents and a great-aunt in Norfolk. Philip's grandfather was a **clergyman**, and although the boys did not enjoy church and Sunday School, they liked living in his rambling **rectory** with its huge garden. They also enjoyed rummaging through the parish play costume collection.

Best of all, Philip's grandfather was a wonderful storyteller. He invented exciting tales about local places, giving them intriguing names from cowboy movies and the story-poem, *Hiawatha*. A teacher at Philip's school, Mr Glegg, also read spellbinding stories and poems aloud, such as *The Rime of the Ancient Mariner*. Philip began to wonder if he could be a writer one day.

" Streaked with crimson, blue and yellow, Crested with great eagle feathers."
" The Song of Hiawatha."—*Longfellow.*

The Song of Hiawatha was written by Henry Wadsworth Longfellow in 1858.

Sailing the seven seas

When Philip was eight years old, his mother remarried. His new stepfather was also a pilot in the RAF, who was soon sent to a base in Australia. Once again, Philip found himself voyaging around the world by ocean liner, the way everyone travelled long distances in those days. During the journey, both Philip and Francis were unlucky enough to come down with a nasty illness called scarlet fever. Confined to their cabin, they built forts and castles from a kit and spent days acting out battles between good and evil forces.

FIND OUT MORE...

Philip has said: "There's nothing like setting out on a long voyage, and beginning a long story is like that … There's a large world in front of you … You're going to go exploring…"

Aeroplane travel was not common when Philip was a boy. People travelled on ocean liners, and the journeys took many weeks.

Life down under

In Australia, Philip came across comic books for the first time. These featured superheroes such as Batman and Superman, and told stories in an entirely new combination of words and pictures. Philip also decided that the Australian children's classic *The Magic Pudding* by Norman Lindsay was the funniest book he had ever read. He made up his mind that he definitely wanted to be a storyteller more than anything else.

Australian radio inspired Philip to invent his own tales. One of his favourite radio shows was about a kangaroo that kept repair tools in its pouch and had all sorts of adventures. Every night, when Philip and his brother were tucked up in bed, Philip would sing the kangaroo show's theme tune, then make up his own adventure.

Putting down roots

When Philip was ten, the family moved back to Britain. His mother had had another son and a daughter, and his stepfather resigned from the RAF to work as a **civilian** pilot. They settled in Llanbedr in North Wales, in a hillside house surrounded by woods. Philip loved the wild countryside and spent days exploring. He adored ghost stories and scared his brother and friends by making up his own spinechillers about a tree they called "the Hanging Tree". Besides reading ghost stories, Philip enjoyed the *Moomin* books of Tove Jansson, the *Swallows and Amazons* novels of Arthur Ransome, and story called *A Hundred Million Francs* by Paul Berna. Philip was also passionate about poetry.

A Hundred Million Francs is a story about a group of children who find some hidden money. Philip was inspired by this picture, and he says that it helped him create the character of Lyra Belacqua many years later.

Teenage years

As Philip grew older, he liked to spend free time painting and playing the guitar. He also read books such as the *Sherlock Holmes* stories of Arthur Conan Doyle, Homer's *Iliad* and *Odyssey*, and *The Picture History of Painting* by H.W. and D.J. Janson. Philip loved the poetry of Dylan Thomas and John Donne, and spent hours creating his own poems, experimenting endlessly with the rhythm of words.

Philip was encouraged in his writing and reading by a wonderful English teacher named Enid Jones at his secondary school in Harlech. Philip has kept in touch with Enid to this day, and sends her a copy of each new book he has published.

FIND OUT MORE...

Enid Jones introduced Philip to John Milton's mighty poem, *Paradise Lost*. It had a great effect on him, and is where he came across the phrase "his dark materials".

Here Philip is giving copies of his books to the teachers at his old school.

STUDENT AND TEACHER

At the age of eighteen, Philip became the first pupil from his school ever to go to Oxford University. He even won an entrance exam award called a **scholarship**. Looking back, Philip wishes he had gone to art school instead of university. He thought his English course at Oxford was a let-down. There was only one hour a week on the timetable for discussion of all the hundreds of books he had to read. However, he loved the beautiful, ancient city itself. Philip also enjoyed acting in drama groups, playing his guitar, and singing folk songs.

INSIDE INFORMATION

A favourite writer Philip studied at university was William Blake. His books include *The Marriage of Heaven and Hell*, *Songs of Innocence* and *Songs of Experience*.

William Blake was an artist as well as a writer. Philip also enjoys creating illustrations for his own books.

This is the part of Oxford University where Philip studied, called Exeter College.

Work in progress

During his last year at university, Philip came across *The Master and Margarita* by Mikhail Bulgakov. The story was about the devil and his servants arriving in Moscow. Philip only read the description on the back of the book, but this struck a chord – he knew he wanted to write stories that mixed everyday life with fantastic ideas.

The day after finishing his university exams in 1968, Philip started writing a novel. However, he also had to make a living. Philip worked at a famous men's clothes shop in London called Moss Bros, and then he became an assistant librarian. All the time he continued to write. He also got married in 1970, to a teacher named Jude. Philip decided that he could also be a teacher while continuing to write. So he went to college in Weymouth for a year and obtained a teaching qualification.

Settling down

Philip and Jude settled in Oxford, where they have lived ever since. They went on to have two sons, Jamie and Tom. Philip gave up on his first novel, but his second won a competition for young writers – although today Philip thinks it is total rubbish! This was a thriller for adults called *The Haunted Storm*. It was published in 1972, the same year that Philip began teaching English to middle-school children.

Back to school

Philip discovered that he taught best through storytelling. He used ancient **myths** and classic tales such as Homer's *Iliad* and *Odyssey* to examine language, characters, plots and **themes**, and how these related to real life. This inspired him to write a book on **ancient civilizations**, which was published in 1978.

Homer's *Iliad* and *Odyssey* are dramatic tales of war, heroes, gods, and goddesses.

Success!

Philip was still writing fiction, and in 1978 he had an adult **science-fiction** novel published, called *Galatea*. He was also busy creating school plays. These were larger-than-life dramas with wild characters, fantastic scenes, and adventurous plots. Philip had the idea of retelling them as young people's novels. The first, a ghost story called *Count Karlstein*, was published in 1982. The second, a melodrama featuring a sixteen-year-old Victorian orphan called Sally Lockhart, was published in 1985. Titled *The Ruby in the Smoke*, it won the International Reading Association Children's Book Award.

FIND OUT MORE...

A melodrama has an action-packed plot in which a hero and heroine struggle to overcome an evil villain. They were popular entertainment in Victorian times, as theatre plays or as stories for reading aloud to friends. Melodramas were accompanied by music, to help show characters and to raise the level of excitement, danger, and suspense.

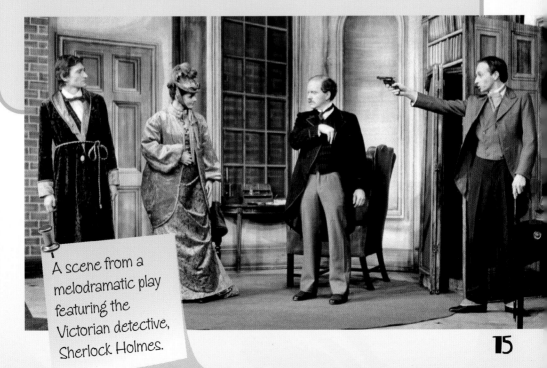

A scene from a melodramatic play featuring the Victorian detective, Sherlock Holmes.

Words, words, words!

One reason why Philip was drawn to writing plays was because he was fascinated with the way people speak, and recreating this in his **dialogue**. Listening to teenagers talking inspired Philip to begin his next book: *How To Be Cool* – the plot grew out of the language, as Philip thought about how some words, phrases and conversation subjects were "in" and some were "out". Philip was as comfortable with Victorian dialogue as with modern-day speech, and in 1986 he wrote another Sally Lockhart story, *The Shadow in the Plate* (which was later retitled *The Shadow in the North*).

HAVE A GO

If you would like to write like Philip, try thinking up a modern-day character and a Victorian character. What might they say to each other if they somehow met? Write out their conversation and then read it aloud with a friend. Do you think it sounds realistic?

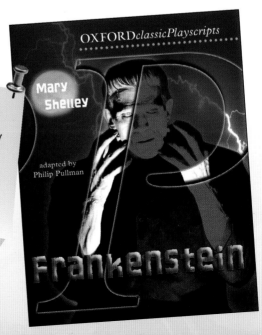

Philip turned the famous 19th-century novel *Frankenstein*, by Mary Shelley, into a script for a play.

OXFORD*classicPlayscripts*

Mary Shelley

adapted by Philip Pullman

Frankenstein

The Polka Theatre was the first theatre in the United Kingdom that was just for children when it opened in 1979.

Teaching teachers

Philip's books were selling well enough for him to work part-time instead of full-time, teaching student teachers at Westminster College, Oxford. They explored creative writing ideas and how to use all sorts of literature in the classroom, including Victorian novels, folk tales, ancient myths and poems, and picture books.

Philip had more time for his own writing, such as *Spring-Heeled Jack* (1989). He created another Sally Lockhart story, called *The Tiger in the Well* (1990), and a story based on characters from the Sally Lockhart books, *The Tin Princess* (1994). He wrote two very different, contemporary novels: *The Broken Bridge* (1990) and *The White Mercedes* (1992, later retitled *The Butterfly Tattoo*). Philip also wrote plays for the Polka Theatre in Wimbledon, London, based on Mary Shelley's *Frankenstein* and Arthur Conan Doyle's *Sherlock Holmes*.

17

Creating modern classics

In 1993, Philip began work on a trilogy of novels, called *His Dark Materials*. This was even more inventive, and much more ambitious, than anything he had previously written. He imagined different universes, sometimes similar in many ways to ours, but also with many magical differences. Philip involved exciting ideas from literature, science, and religion. He worked with many linked plot lines and different layers of meaning.

When the first novel, *Northern Lights*, was published in 1995, it amazed readers and critics worldwide. It won several major book awards and flew off the bookshelves in such huge quantities that Philip was able to give up teaching to concentrate on writing full-time.

These are pictures from two of the chapter headings in *Northern Lights*.

Telling tales

His Dark Materials took seven years to complete. However, Philip continued writing shorter tales at the same time. He created more Victorian adventures, about a group of characters called "the New Cut Gang". *Thunderbolt's Waxwork* was published in 1994 and *The Gas-Fitters' Ball* in 1995. He also wrote several fairy stories. Some were original tales, such as *The Firework-Maker's Daughter* (1995) and *Clockwork* (1996). Others were inspired by existing tales, for instance, *I Was a Rat!* (1999) sprang from *Cinderella*.

HAVE A GO

Philip's top tips for budding writers are:
- Read, read, and read some more!
- Find somewhere relaxing to write and do not always worry about planning first.
- Do not try to write what other people tell you to write. Write what you want to write, how you want to write it.

John Lawrence drew illustrations for *Lyra's Oxford*, a book linked to the *His Dark Materials* trilogy.

Philip has used his memories of living in the beautiful countryside of North Wales in his writing.

Inspiration from real life

Philip's writing is very imaginative. He does not base his characters on himself or people he knows; he invents them all. Philip is especially good at dreaming up courageous girls, such as Sally Lockhart and Lyra Belacqua, outsize villains such as Count Karlstein and Mrs Coulter, and mythical, magical creatures, such as armoured bears and Gallivespians.

However, Philip does use settings familiar to him. For instance, he put the Welsh countryside he knew in his teenage years in *The Broken Bridge*. And he used his home city of Oxford as a basis for the parallel worlds in *His Dark Materials*. Philip also looks to his interests for inspiration, such as the Victorian era and cutting-edge science. He has also put his personal thoughts about religion into his work.

Ideas from other stories

Philip has said that he has stolen ideas from every book he has ever read. He sometimes makes it apparent if he has particular writers and works in mind by including quotations from them in his stories. Other times, he leaves you the pleasure of spotting individual influences for yourself! Many different general styles of book have also inspired him. For instance, comic books led him to experiment with the way drawings can help tell a story, in the graphic novel versions of *Count Karlstein* and *Spring-Heeled Jack*.

Philip has also used ancient **narrative forms** such as the "story within a story" – a device which dates back to the *Arabian Nights* and beyond. He always adds plenty of his own original ideas – which Philip says he gets by sitting quietly for a long time and thinking hard!

INSIDE INFORMATION

Philip thinks that one of his best ideas was that of dæmons – the animal **familiars** people have in *His Dark Materials*. You cannot choose your own dæmon; it is a reflection of your true nature which is changeable during childhood but becomes fixed during **adolescence**. Philip suspects that his dæmon would be a jackdaw or a magpie, because he likes collecting unusual objects which catch his eye. What do you think your dæmon might be? Your friends may have some interesting suggestions.

Being Philip Pullman

Today, as a best-selling, world-famous author, Philip is kept extremely busy giving interviews and talks, appearing on television and radio, and meeting his fans at schools, libraries, and bookshops. On days when he has time to write, he begins at around half-past nine in the morning and works until lunchtime. Afterwards, he watches *Neighbours* and spends the afternoon drawing, making things out of wood, or practising his piano-playing.

INSIDE INFORMATION

Philip loves dictionaries and reference books of any sort, but particularly those to do with language. He sometimes flicks through books like this to help him invent characters' names. He got the name Serafina Pekkala, a witch in *His Dark Materials*, from flicking through a telephone directory from Helsinki in Finland!

Philip finds it fascinating to watch how the storylines of the television soap *Neighbours* unfold week after week.

Philip used to work in a shed, like the author Roald Dahl.

Philip's space

For years, Philip worked in a big shed at the bottom of his garden. He had a writing table and chair in there, with a comfy armchair. The shed was filled with dust, cobwebs and rubbish, and was overflowing with piles and piles of books, stacks of jiffy bags, heaps of manuscripts and drawings, and all sorts of writing equipment. But it also had lots of interesting items, which Philip has around him to stimulate his writing, such as a six-foot long stuffed rat from one of his Sherlock Holmes plays, masks, a saxophone, and stones from Prague and Mont Blanc. Now Philip has moved to a big house with a large, indoor study. This is where he keeps his power tools, two guitars, an accordion, and all his treasured possessions, as well as where he does his writing.

PHILIP'S WORK

Ever since Philip began writing, he has worked on his stories every day. He writes **longhand**, using a ballpoint pen on narrow-lined A4 paper. He makes sure he completes three pages every day, which is about 1,100 words. Then he stops – but not before he has written the first sentence on the next page, so he never has to begin the following morning with a blank page facing him. When he finishes a story, he types it up on a computer.

Philip now works in a comfortable study with a big window.

Thinking in pictures

Philip does not start a story by thinking of an idea or a theme. Instead, he nearly always begins from a picture that pops into his head from nowhere. *His Dark Materials* began with a picture of a little girl overhearing something she wasn't supposed to overhear.

Philip jots down the pictures he sees in his mind's eye on yellow sticky notes. He thinks about what might connect them together, and writes brief sentences on other stickies summarising more possible scenes. Then he sticks all the notes – often fifty or sixty – on a huge piece of paper, and moves them all around to get the best order. This way, Philip creates the outline of a story, although he has not thought about any detail. When he starts writing, his characters develop lives of their own and the story takes itself off in new, exciting directions.

Finishing touches

Philip reworks a story many times before he is finally happy with it. But he thinks you can "polish a story so hard it vanishes under the gloss". He says that the best stories are like paintings in which you can see the brushstrokes – they show the energy and life of the human hand that is behind them, along with a few rough edges here and there!

FIND OUT MORE...

Philip has a very visual imagination. His sheet of sticky notes works rather like an artist's storyboard. Some of Philip's favourite illustrators include Peter Bailey, Ian Beck, and John Lawrence, all of whom he has had the honour of working with. Philip drew the illustrations that were used with the chapter headings in the first two books of *His Dark Materials* himself. You can see two of them on page 18 of this book.

COUNT KARLSTEIN

Main characters

Count Karlstein .... an evil villain
Arturo Snivelwurst ..... the Count's manservant
Lucy and Charlotte .... Count Karlstein's orphan nieces
Hildi .... a good-hearted maidservant in
                        Count Karlstein's castle
Peter .... Hildi's brother, who is in hiding
                        from the police for suspected poaching
Augusta Davenport ... a plucky Englishwoman, a teacher
                        from Lucy and Charlotte's old school
Eliza .... Augusta's maid
Dr Cadaverezzi .... an amazing conjuror
Max .... Dr Cadaverezzi's assistant and Eliza's
                        long-lost **fiancé**

Sergeant Snitsch
   and Constable
   Winkelburg .... two bumbling policemen
Meister Haifisch .... a cool, calm and collected lawyer
Zamiel .... the Demon Huntsman

The plot

The scene is snowy Switzerland, the year is 1816. The dastardly
Count Karlstein lives in a castle high above Karlstein village. He has
made a terrible bargain with Zamiel, the Demon Huntsman. In return
for money and status, the Count has forfeited the lives of his own
neices, Lucy and Charlotte – unbeknown to them. It will soon be All
Souls' Eve, when Zamiel will be coming to collect his terrible prize.

When the girls go missing, the desperate Count is thrown into a hunt of his own. It is not an easy search – the village is bustling with visitors who have arrived for a shooting contest; the mysterious magician, Dr Cadaverezzi, is creating havoc; and the girls' former teacher, Miss Davenport, is determined to get to the bottom of their disappearance herself. The local police do not know which way to turn! Will anyone rescue Lucy and Charlotte – or will they meet a terrible fate?

INSIDE INFORMATION

In *Count Karlstein*, Philip has added his comic flair to the gothic horror tales which were popular in the 18th and 19th centuries. These scary stories were atmospheric, suspenseful thrillers, set in far-flung places. They often included ruined castles and crumbling mansions, full of mysterious, **macabre** goings on, curses and superstitions, and supernatural hauntings.

The story *Count Karlstein* was published as a book in 1982.

THE FIREWORK-MAKER'S DAUGHTER

Main characters

Lalchand.................... a Firework-Maker
Lila............................ the Firework-Maker's daughter
Chulak....................... Lila's friend, and personal servant
                                   to Hamlet
Hamlet .... the King's White Elephant – whom
                                   only Chulak and Lila know can talk
Ravanzi..................... the terrifying Fire-Fiend
the Goddess of the
    Emerald Lake .... who helps Lila
Rambashi .... an ex-chicken-farmer, turned chief
                                   of the River Pirates, turned restaurant-
                                   owner, turned singing group leader

Dr Puffenflasch,
    Signor Scorcini,
    and Colonel Sam
    Sparkington .... Firework-Makers
the King.................... who holds Lila's father's life in his hands

The plot

Lila lives "a thousand miles ago, in a country east of the jungle and south of the mountains". More than anything else in the world, she wants to be a Firework-Maker like her father. But her father tells a secret to her friend, Chulak. Every Firework-Maker must travel to the Grotto of Razvani, the Fire-Fiend, and bring back some Royal Sulphur – an ingredient which makes the best fireworks.

The determined Lila undertakes a perilous journey, only to find that there is no such thing as Royal Sulphur, and that her actions have led to her father being thrown into prison and sentenced to death. The King agrees to spare Lila's father – but only if he and Lila can together win a competition between the finest Firework-Makers in the land.

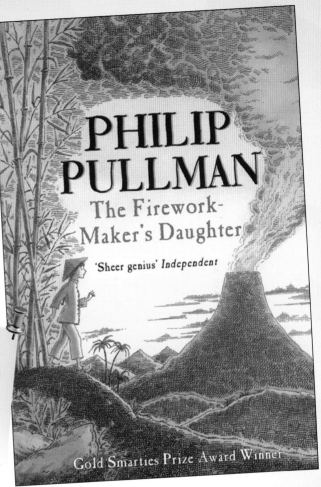

The Firework-Maker's Daughter was published in 1995.

INSIDE INFORMATION

Philip has said that the idea for *The Firework-Maker's Daughter* came from his childhood when, every Guy Fawkes' Night, his family held their own firework display. Philip was captivated by the exploding, colourful bursts of stars, with their bangs, whizzes and whooshes, but he loved the exciting names of the fireworks just as much. In *The Firework-Maker's Daughter*, he gave himself the chance to make up his own names, including Java Lights, Crackle-Dragons, Golden Sneezes, and Tumbling Demons.

CLOCKWORK

Main characters

Karl .... **apprentice** to the clockmaker of Glockenheim

Fritz .... the town storyteller

Gretl .... a kind, brave **taverner's** daughter

Dr Kalmenius .... a clockwork-maker so famous that stories are told far and wide about him and his amazing creations.

Prince Otto and Princess Mariposa ... about whom, Fritz tells a story

Prince Florian.............. the Prince and Princess's clockwork son, who needs a human heart to survive

Sir Ironsoul .... an amazing but sinister clockwork figure of a knight in armour

The plot

One snowy night, in a tavern in a small German town of Glockenheim, Fritz starts to tell his new story: a macabre tale of a tragic little prince and the magical clockworkmaker, Dr Kalmenius. Before Fritz has a chance to finish, the tavern door opens and in walks – Dr Kalmenius himself! He has come on a long journey to witness the unveiling of a new figure for the famous moving clock of Glockenheim. But Karl, the clockmaker's apprentice who is responsible for creating the new figure, has failed to invent anything.

Dr Kalmenius leaves Karl with what seems to be the perfect solution: a clockwork knight called Sir Ironsoul, who moves at the word "devil" and stops at a secret whistle. Then the taverner's daughter, Gretl, comes across another perfect clockwork model, of a tragic little prince. She realizes that something very strange is afoot. The secret can only lie with Fritz and his story.

PHILIP PULLMAN
Clockwork
or All Wound Up

'Exciting, scary, romantic and deliciously readable'
Guardian

Clockwork was published in 1996.

THE "SALLY LOCKHART" NOVELS

Main characters

Sally Lockhart........... a courageous young orphan woman

Jim Taylor .... Sally's close friend – an office-boy turned melodrama-writer and private detective

Frederick Garland .... a London photographer, with whom Sally falls in love and sets up a business

Mrs Holland.............. an opium-house owner set on acquiring a precious treasure

Mr Mackinnon .... a music-hall magician and psychic, with a secret love

Axel Bellmann .... a rich financier

Ah Ling .... real name: Hendrik van Eeden – dastardly member of a secret society called The Seven Blessings

Dan Goldberg .... a good-hearted man whose mission in life is to improve life for poor and powerless people in Victorian society

Sarah-Jane Russell ... nurse to Sally's daughter, Harriet, secretly in love with Jim Taylor

The plots

The Ruby in the Smoke is the first novel featuring Sally Lockhart. She is on a quest to understand a mysterious message left to her when the man she believes was her father died in the South China Sea. Sally finds herself caught up in a dangerous **intrigue** involving letters, opium, and a priceless jewel. Luckily, she finds courageous friends to help her fend off the evil villains who surround her.

In *The Shadow in the North*, Sally has become a financial consultant. A shipping business which she had recommended as an investment has strangely failed, so Sally sets about investigating. She uncovers fraud, murder, and the manufacture of a secret war machine. Sally and her friends place themselves continually in peril, to the great cost of one of them.

In *The Tiger in the Well*, Sally is bringing up a daughter, Harriet, on her own. Out of the blue, she receives a petition for divorce – even though she has never been married! Under the Victorian legal system, Sally stands to lose everything – including her daughter.

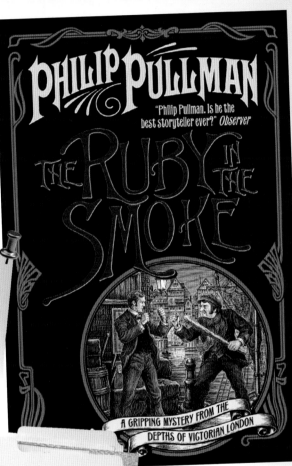

The Ruby in the Smoke was published in 1985.

PHILIP PULLMAN

"Philip Pullman. Is he the best storyteller ever?" *Observer*

THE RUBY IN THE SMOKE

A GRIPPING MYSTERY FROM THE DEPTHS OF VICTORIAN LONDON

INSIDE INFORMATION

The "Sally Lockhart" novels focus attention on many Victorian social issues, such as mass poverty, drug-taking, scandal over unmarried mothers, and the powerlessness of women in the eyes of the law. However, Philip writes about this gritty **realism** in the theatrical, comical style of Victorian melodrama, with braver-than-brave heroes and heroines; dastardly, cloaked villains; fortunate and unfortunate coincidences; and just-in-the-nick-of-time escapes.

HIS DARK MATERIALS

Main characters

Lyra Belacqua .... a girl who lives in another world, in a place similar to Oxford in our world (she is later given the name Silvertongue)

Pantalaimon.............. Lyra's dæmon (an animal **familiar** – a constant companion)

Lord Asriel .... a scholar and politician, Lyra's father

Mrs Coulter .... a church leader, Lyra's mother

Iorek Byrnison .... an armoured polar bear

Lee Scoresby .... a Texan hot-air balloonist

Serafina Pekkala....... queen of a witch clan

the gyptians .... boat-people, Lyra's friends

Will Parry .... a twelve-year-old boy from our world

Dr Mary Malone....... a scientist in our world conducting experiments into what she calls "Shadows" – what people in Lyra's world know as "Dust"

The plot

Philip has described *His Dark Materials* as one story in three parts. *Northern Lights* focuses on Lyra, who lives in a world similar to ours. She hears talk of this parallel world and of "Dust" – invisible particles which gather around human beings. She is determined to find a number of children who have mysteriously gone missing, and in doing so, uncovers an evil Church plot.

The Subtle Knife starts in our world, and tells how Will Parry stumbles through a window in the air to Cittagazze, an eerie place between millions of different worlds. There he meets Lyra, and becomes embroiled in her struggle against the forces of evil.

At the beginning of *The Amber Spyglass*, Will and Lyra have been split up. Representatives from the Church are hunting out Lyra to kill her – but the determined Will finds her first. Together, they make a treacherous journey to the underworld of the dead. Finally, their fight to establish good, justice and truth in the universe requires them to make a terrible sacrifice.

INSIDE INFORMATION

Even though the story features different universes and many imaginary creatures, Philip insists that *His Dark Materials* are "stark realism" rather than fantasy. He means that the main focus of his novels is on the experience of growing up, rather than on witches, wizards, and magic.

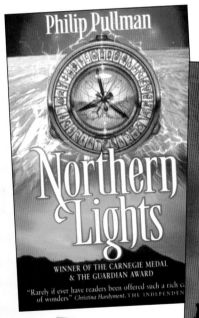

Northern Lights was published in 1995, The Subtle Knife in 1997, and The Amber Spyglass in 2000.

PRIZES, POINTS OF VIEW, AND PERFORMANCE

Philip has won many prizes for his work, including these major awards:

- *The Firework-Maker's Daughter* won a Gold Medal at the Smarties Book Awards.
- *Clockwork* won a Silver Medal at the Smarties Book Awards and was **shortlisted** for the two most prestigious prizes in the book publishing industry: the Carnegie Medal and the Whitbread Children's Book Award.
- *Northern Lights* won both the Carnegie Medal and the Guardian Children's Fiction Award, and was named Children's Book of the Year at the British Book Awards.
- *The Amber Spyglass* won not just the children's section at the Whitbread Book Awards but also the overall, main prize – the Whitbread Book of the Year (2001). It was the first children's story ever to beat all the books for adults.

The Carnegie Medal is one of the top awards for children's writers.

FIND OUT MORE...

Philip thinks that stories are crucially important. He says: "they entertain and teach; they help us both enjoy life and endure it. After nourishment, shelter and companionship, stories are the thing we need most in the world."

Here Philip is giving a speech to accept the Whitbread Book of the Year award.

Special honours

In 2002, the book publishing world gave Philip a prize called the Eleanor Farjeon Award. This was because his stories had changed the opinion of many people who had previously thought that children's books were second-rate writing compared to books for adults.

In 2004, the Queen honoured Philip by making him a Commander of the Order of the British Empire. He now has letters after his name, and his full title is Philip Pullman CBE. Philip went to Buckingham Palace to receive his CBE medal from the Queen herself.

In 2005, Philip won the Astrid Lindgren Memorial Award. This is the world's largest award for writers and illustrators of books for young people, and was awarded to Philip for the whole of his work rather than one individual book.

Cause for controversy

No one can deny that Philip has outstanding storytelling skills. However, his ideas have caused a commotion. *His Dark Materials* created a scandal among many Christians worldwide, because the story goes against their religious beliefs and the authority of the Church. Philip does not think there is any proof that God exists. He thinks that throughout history, people have often used **organized religion** as an excuse to do cruel and unjust things.

However, Philip is not simply an "anti-Christian writer" as some people have claimed. In the "Sally Lockhart" novels, Philip also paints other social institutions as dishonourable and unhelpful. Philip says that his stories are just that: tales – full of imagination and ideas. He does not write them to put across arguments or as **propaganda** designed to change people's opinions.

Philip had a debate with the Archbishop of Canterbury about God and religion.

The National Theatre production of *His Dark Materials* brought the story and characters to life.

On stage and screen

How to be Cool and *I Was A Rat!* have been acted on television. *His Dark Materials* has also been read on radio, performed as a play at the National Theatre in London, and made into films for television and the big screen. Other professional writers work on these fantastic adaptations, because Philip is always too busy writing his next book.

HAVE A GO

HAVE A GO

How would you turn one of Philip's stories into a play?
- Break up your action and dialogue into scenes in different settings.
- You could work in order from the beginning to the end, or include "flashback" scenes to show the past.
- Your characters might occasionally talk to the audience, or you could use a **narrator**.
- Give instructions to tell the actors how to speak and move.
- Think about special effects, stunts, and music.

Views in the news

When you are a famous author like Philip, people called critics write their opinions of your work for newspapers and magazines. These are known as book reviews, and they help readers decide whether to spend their time and money on a story or not. Here's an example of a review for *Spring-Heeled Jack*, with some notes on how the critic has put it together. Would it encourage you to read the book?

If you could go back in time and ask any Victorian who they think is the greatest crime-fighter of all time, they'd scoff at Superman … they'd sniff at Batman … they'd say: Spring-heeled Jack! But can the superhero combat supervillain Mack the Knife? You'll find out in this escapade, which tells of three children trying to escape from a terrible fate at an orphanage.

a little about the story without giving too much away

Philip Pullman is the author of the best-selling, Carnegie-medal winning trilogy *His Dark Materials*. He is a master of stories set in the murky back streets of old London town, such as the "Sally Lockhart" novels and the "New Cut Gang" stories. *Spring-Heeled Jack* has all the entertaining elements of Victorian melodrama: brave heroes and heroines, love-to-hate villains, bumbling policemen – and more twists and turns and cliff-hangers in the plot than a rollercoaster!

some background information about the author

comparision with other works

the critic's opinion on whether it is a good or bad read, with clear reasons

Spring-Heeled Jack is a fantastic adventure told not only in words but also in cartoons, making it hugely enjoyable for readers of eight and over.

a recommendation of who the critic thinks will like the book

HAVE A GO

Why not try writing your own review of a Philip Pullman book? You could give it to a friend who does not know the story and see if they go on to read it. Ask them to write a review back, recommending one of their own favourite reads to you. You might discover a great new book, poem, or writer...

Pieces of praise

Here are some critics' opinions about Philip and his work:

"Philip Pullman, one of the supreme literary dreamers and magicians of our time."

The Guardian

"Philip Pullman. Is he the best storyteller ever?"

The Observer

"Philip Pullman, capable of lighting up the dullest day or greyest spirit with the incandescence of his imagination."

Nicholas Tucker in The Independent

On *His Dark Materials*:

"A genuine masterpiece of intelligent, imaginative storytelling..."

The Mail on Sunday

On *His Dark Materials*: "...should please all ages from eight to eighty."

Top author, Nina Bawden

"*His Dark Materials* stands revealed as one of the most important children's books of our time."

The Daily Telegraph

LONG LIVE PHILIP PULLMAN!

If you would like to find out more about Philip and his work, he often gives talks at bookshops and at literary festivals. He has been the subject of television programmes, such as *The World of Philip Pullman* in 2002 and the *South Bank Show* in 2003, and a guest on radio programmes such as *Desert Island Discs*.

Philip's future plans

Philip has already written a huge variety of books, so it will be fascinating to see what he writes in the future. He will almost certainly create new books based on *His Dark Materials*, and he says that he has plenty more Sally Lockhart stories in his head. One thing is for sure: Philip will continue writing for as long as he is able. He has said that if storytelling suddenly became a crime, he would break the law without a moment's hesitation!

Philip has signed thousands of books for his fans around the world.

Writing in focus

Philip has millions of fans worldwide. Here is what some of them think about him and his work:

"I love Sally Lockhart. I wish I could meet her!"

Emma, aged eleven, from Edinburgh

"Philip Pullman villains are wickedly wicked!"

Owen, aged ten, from Cardiff

"If I could only ever read three books again for the rest of my life, I'd choose the His Dark Materials trilogy."

Claire, aged twelve, from Cornwall

PHILIP'S WISH LIST

Hopes... Philip can never seem to draw or paint people's faces as he wants them. He hopes he will be able to crack this special skill one day.

Dreams... When Philip was young, he dreamed of being an author. He is delighted that his dream has come true.

Ambitions... Philip has an ambition to write and illustrate a picture book all by himself. Other than that, he just wants to keep doing what he is doing, for as long as possible – lucky for us!

TIMELINE

1946 Philip is born on October 19.

1954 Philip's father is killed in Africa. The family return to England.

1955 Philip's mother remarries and the family move to Australia.

1957 Philip's family move to Llanbedr, North Wales.

1964 Philip studies English at Exeter College, Oxford University.

1968 Philip starts writing novels while doing different jobs in London.

1970 Philip gets married to Jude.

1971 Philip studies in Weymouth for a teaching certificate.

1972 Philip and Jude settle in Oxford, where they have two sons.
Philip begins teaching English to middle-school children.
The Haunted Storm, a thriller for adults, is published.

1978 Philip has an ancient history book published, and also
a science-fiction novel for adults called *Galatea*.
He begins creating exciting, adventure-filled school plays.

1982 One of Philip's school plays, *Count Karlstein*, is published
as a story.

1985 *The Ruby in the Smoke* is published.

1986 *The Shadow in the North* is published.

1987 *How To Be Cool* is published.

1988 Philip starts teaching part-time at Westminster College, Oxford.
Philip begins writing plays for the Polka Children's Theatre.
The Ruby in the Smoke wins the International Reading Association
Children's Book Award.

1989 *Spring-Heeled Jack* is published.

1990 *The Tiger in the Well*, *The Broken Bridge*, and a play adaptation
of *Frankenstein* are published.

1992 *The White Mercedes* (later retitled *The Butterfly Tattoo*) and
Sherlock Holmes: A Play are published.

1993 Philip begins work on the books which will become *His Dark
Materials*.

1993 *The Wonderful Story of Aladdin and the Enchanted Lamp* is published.

1994 *The Tin Princess* and *Thunderbolt's Waxwork* are published.

1995 *Northern Lights* and *The Firework-Maker's Daughter* are published (in the United States, *Northern Lights* is titled *The Golden Compass*).

1996 Philip gives up teaching.
Clockwork is published.
Northern Lights wins the Guardian Children's Fiction Award and the Carnegie Medal and is named as the Children's Book of the Year at the British Book Awards.
The Firework-Maker's Daughter wins a Gold Medal at the Smarties Book Awards.

1997 *The Subtle Knife* is published.
Clockwork wins a Silver Medal at the Smarties Book Awards and is shortlisted for the Carnegie Medal and the Whitbread Children's Book Award.

1998 *The Gas Fitter's Ball* and *Mossycoat* are published.

1999 *I Was a Rat!* is published.

2000 *The Amber Spyglass* and *Puss in Boots* are published.

2001 *The Amber Spyglass* wins the Whitbread Book of the Year
A play called *Sherlock Holmes and the Limehouse horror* is published.

2002 Philip wins the Eleanor Farjeon Award.

2003 *Lyra's Oxford* is published.

2004 The Queen awards Philip a CBE.
The Scarecrow and His Servant is published.

2005 Philip is awarded the Astrid Lindgren Memorial Award – the world's largest award for writers of books for young people.

FURTHER RESOURCES

More books to read

Darkness Visible: Inside the World of Philip Pullman, Nicholas Tucker (Wizard Books 2003)

Philip Pullman's His Dark Materials Trilogy: A Reader's Guide, Claire Squires (Continuum, 2003)

The Science of Philip Pullman's His Dark Materials, John and Mary Gribbin (Hodder Children's Books, 2004)

Audiobooks

Versions of many of Philip's stories are also available as audiobooks on CD and cassette, including:

His Dark Materials Trilogy: BBC Radio 4 (Full-cast Dramatization), (BBC Audiobooks, 2003)

Lyra's Oxford (Random House Children's Books Audio CD, 2003)

Websites

Philip's own personal website:
www.philip-pullman.com

Unofficial website dedicated to the *His Dark Materials* trilogy:
www.hisdarkmaterials.org

A site all about books for young people:
www.booktrusted.co.uk

Disclaimer

All the internet addresses (URLs) given in this book were valid at the time of going to press. However, due to the dynamic nature of the Internet, some addresses may have changed, or sites may have ceased to exist since publication. While the author and publishers regret any inconvenience this may cause readers, no responsibility for any such changes can be accepted by either the author or the publishers.

adolescence time when people change from a child into an adult

ancient civilizations societies of people who lived many years ago, such as the Romans and Greeks

apprentice person learning a trade from a skilled worker

civilian regular member of the public

clergyman someone who is a minister for the Christian church

contemporary modern in style

dialogue speech or conversation

familiar spirit of a person in animal form

fiancé male who is engaged to be married

gothic horror form of story based on horror and mystery

graphic novel type of book where the story is told in pictures

intrigue mysterious events that are difficult to figure out

lodgings place someone lives in but does not own

longhand writing on paper with a pen or pencil rather than typing

macabre gruesome, ghastly, grim

melodrama story and play form where a hero or heroine struggles against larger-than-life villains

myth traditional story from early history, typically about gods, goddesses, spirits, and heroes

mythic relating to stories about the believed history of gods, godesses, spirits, and heroes

narrative form method of telling a story

narrator person who tells a story

organized religion large system of faith such as Islam, Christianity, Judaism, Sikhism, Hinduism

propaganda information designed specifically to change people's opinions in a certain way

realism relating to real-life events

rectory house where a rector lives. A rector is a particular type of clergyman.

scholarship prize given to a student to help them pay for a course of study

science fiction story based on real science and technology but with made-up elements, often set in a different time or place

shortlist final list of candidates for an award, from which the winner is selected

taverner historical term for a person who runs a tavern (public house)

theme idea explored in detail by an author

trilogy series of three things which are related, for example stories using the same characters

INDEX

Titles in the *Writers Uncovered* series include:

HB   0 431 90626 2

HB   0 431 90627 0

HB   0 431 90628 9

HB   0 431 90629 7

HB   0 431 90630 0

HB   0 431 90631 9

HB   0 431 90632 7

HB   0 431 90633 5

Find out about other titles from Heinemann Library on our website www.heinemann.co.uk/library

Also available from Heinemann Literature:

Hardback   0 435 23339 4

Find out about other titles from Heinemann Literature on our website www.heinemann.co.uk/literature